HOPE & HELP FOR YOUR JOB SEARCH

Sane Advice From An Employment Professional

L. T. Buck

Copyright © 2014 L. T. Buck
All rights reserved.
ISBN: 978-1-496-12312-1

All rights reserved. No part of this book may be reproduced or transmitted in any form or by any means, electronic or mechanical, including photocopying, recording, or any information storage and retrieval system without prior written permission of the author. Your support of author's rights is appreciated.

TABLE OF CONTENTS

Table Of Contents i
Introduction 1
Chapter One...3
Chapter 2 9
Chapter 3 20
Chapter 4 30
Chapter 5 33
Chapter 6 37
Chapter 7 52
Chapter 8 61
Chapter 9 78
Chapter 10 86
List of Job Seeker Resources..89

INTRODUCTION

Job searching can feel a lot like being stranded in the middle of a vast frozen lake: a mind-numbing, soul-crushing, spirit-breaking exercise in emotional torture, with no rescue or help in sight.

Job searching is real life, not a first grade tee ball game. Not everyone gets a trophy. If you have barriers, like a spotty employment history, no education, or other issues, it can seem downright impossible. And the older you are, the proportionately worse it feels. I've added a special chapter at the end for those of you in this group.

You are not hopeless, and you are not alone. Whether you are starting from scratch, a housewife out of the work world for a decade, over fifty and suddenly unemployed, under twenty-one with no job history or re-entering life after prison, there is a place for you. Getting to that place involves work you can do yourself, at home, starting now - developing self-awareness about the person you are now, and what that person needs to adjust in order to become employed.

I suppose you're wondering: who is this know-it-all who thinks they can fix MY life? I don't know everything, but I've been where you are now.

Unemployed, full of anxiety, no cash coming in, with no idea how to start.

I can't fix your life, but I can help you get a job. I might not always tell you things you want to hear, but I will tell you the truth.

As an employment services professional, I've helped hundreds of adults and teens from all kinds of backgrounds find work through state and county workforce programs. But, this isn't about me. This is about you and your desire for a better life for you and your family.

Chapter One
The Freedom To Change

How did you get here? You're unemployed and job searching. That answer is unique to you and your life. How you arrived at your current situation is only important if you can look back, retrace your steps (and missteps), and gain valuable insights for making future choices and decisions. Even if it was through no fault of your own, you need to move forward.

You cannot change the past.

You can learn from that past, and you can control your future. Your past choices may have gotten you here, but today is a new day. This sounds corny, doesn't it?

It's the truth.

All we have is this new day right in front of us, with all of its possibilities.

Today is the day to look inward, and determine what it is about your life that needs to be different in order for you to become successfully employed. You have the freedom to view yourself in a true, unflinching way.

Own it. The good and not so good. The habits you have that improve your daily life, and those that are harmful.

Recognize and discard your self-sabotaging behaviors. You are free to toss out all of those. You have the freedom to make changes – but change only happens when you are ready. Not your spouse, your parents, or your friends.

How serious are you about taking a good look at whatever is currently standing between you and working? Think about the reasons your last jobs haven't worked out. What can you change?

Maybe you have a bit longer to go on your severance package, unemployment, or cash aid and intend to ride it out until the end. You can buckle down and get a job when you really have to, right? Or, you sort of want to go back to work, but do not intend to accept a job at less than (fill in the blank per hour). Even though you haven't had an interview in ten months. Whatever the situation, you need to arrive at your own conclusions about your work readiness.

If you are not quite ready to work, we are wasting each other's time. Good luck to you.

If you are ready to work, keep reading.

What is work, exactly?

No one ever said, "I wish I'd spent more time at work" on their deathbed.

Nevertheless, we need to work, just the same.

Work is the foundation of a life. A cornerstone. A building block. Think of work as a vehicle taking you where you want to go.

Unemployment and cash aid from welfare are short-term safety nets, and there's never a raise on either. Financial insecurity is scary, but so is dependence.

Envision a future in which all of your other options have expired. No more unemployment payments, no more cash aid, food stamps, subsidized daycare and transportation, or free medical care.

Now envision a future where more people are taking out of the system than putting in. How long can that last? Soon the well runs dry, and there is no more money or help— for anyone.

You are not afraid, because a few years earlier you decided to begin working.

Work is your vehicle taking you toward what you want, but more important, taking you away from what you do NOT want.

Start by choosing to move that vehicle forward. Your starting place is where you are now. Realistically inventory the barriers that are between you and the life you are moving toward, and determine the best course to remove or mitigate those barriers.

Choosing to move forward may mean taking modest steps that will lead to big changes. It may mean taking a job that isn't your first choice or the pay you expect, but every little step generates energy.

Small steps have a way of leading to big positive changes, even if, in the moment, it seems like nothing is happening. Time will pass, regardless. The foundation you build now will support the life you want to have.

You throw a few coins into a piggy bank every day without thinking about it, and one day, you pick it up and it's full.

You stop drinking soda, and three weeks later, your pants fit comfortably for the first time in years. It all adds up, pun intended. Controlling your own life begins with acknowledging that you have the control, and the power to make changes. Even while you are not working, you can control your daily schedule.

You can choose whom you associate with.

You can choose how to spend your time and money.

You can choose what you eat and what you wear.

You can choose where you go.

Make the choices that most benefit you, and help move you toward your goal of employment.

I've suggested some simple written exercises you might find helpful. Activity is important, especially during times of stress. A simple formula I read years ago (on a refrigerator magnet, of all places) ago has served me well:

Activity

Absorbs

Anxiety

It's true.

I've also included some little tidbits called Magic Keys. These are simply things that I have seen work, repeatedly, in helping people progress along the road to meaningful employment.

Suggested Exercise: Get a notebook.

It doesn't need to be fancy, any small or medium-sized lined ring binder or composition notebook will do fine. Use it to keep track of your progress. No one needs to know about it except you, unless you choose to share it. Think about all you need to do in a day. Create your own daily schedule (by create I mean write it down).

How much time should you spend job searching?

Treat it like a job, and work at it at least four hours per day minimum.

Plan to do productive tasks; don't settle for settling in front of the television or computer all day.

Television is an escape, yes, but it is also the source of lots of unhappiness. Television manipulates us into thinking we want or need certain things, or that everyone is out there having a great life except us. Please. Turn that thing off and tune in to what is going on inside your own four walls. There is a person there, with real hopes and dreams. That person is you.

What do you write in this magic notebook?
- What are your goals?
- What is your dream career?
- What realistic jobs could you get that might lead to that career?
- Make a list of three things you can do today that will help move you in that direction.
- If you feel creative and the house is quiet, find a glue stick and some old magazines. Find pictures that express your dreams and reserve one page of that notebook, or even the inside back cover, to create a vision board.

That's the only arts and crafts project, I promise. The idea was to get you thinking, and doing stuff with our hands, (activity) helps get rid of anxiety.

- Think about better ways to organize your life.
- Then do it. Cleaning and getting rid of the excess junk helps clear your mind. Remember, when you are working again, you won't have time for those cleaning projects.
- Break your cleaning/organizing tasks down into bite-sized pieces. By this, for example, I mean make it a goal to clean two chairs (yes, they need cleaning), one desk drawer, and one dresser drawer in a day. In addition, clean one sink. Make it meaningful, and get rid of junk. It feels good.

Now that you've made a start, take the time to show some kindness to yourself. Change the habits that need changing, the ones that are harmful to your body and spirit, and ones that are making you feel rotten. Think of these habits as getting rid of more junk. Out with the old, and in with the new. Take the time to get to know you, physically, mentally, and emotionally.

I highly recommend you read The Four Agreements by Don Miguel Ruiz. It offers a framework for personal change, and the "agreements" will serve you well in the workplace, and in your life.
They are, in brief:
1. Be Impeccable with Your Word
2. Don't Take Anything Personally
3. Don't Make Assumptions
4. Always Do Your Best

People re-invent themselves every day. You're people. You can do it, too.

CHAPTER 2

FACE THE FACTS: PERCEPTION IS REALITY

Thirty seconds.

That's how long it takes a hiring manager or recruiter to determine, in person, whether a job candidate has a shot at the position.

Now for the *bad* news. Once I get to know a hiring manager or recruiter a little better, they usually admit the truth: It's more like *TWO* seconds.

Two seconds to decide if you are right for the job. How can they possibly know so quickly? Yet recruiters that hire large numbers of people swear by it:

"It's intuition, a gut instinct."

"I kind of take in the whole picture at once and get a feeling. It isn't a conscious, deliberate process."

"I just *know*."

One recruiter put it this way: "It's that instant first impression. Positive, negative, or neutral. If it's positive, or even neutral, the rest is up to them in the interview. But negative is fatal. Negative never changes to positive."

And this: "Yes, I've let myself be talked into hiring a candidate when my gut said 'no', and it turned out to be a disaster—I've never done it again."

Believe me, if I could bottle whatever it is that creates that positive first impression, I would. First impressions trump everything: the perfect résumé, the slam-dunk cover letter, the flawless application. So how do you make the most out of those mere seconds of opportunity?

The employment industry word for it is "presentation."

Often a recruiter will call after I've sent over a job seeker's résumé to ask: How do they *present*? Your presentation is the way you look plus the attitude and body language you project—the total package that signals hiring managers and recruiters in a whopping half-minute that you are the one they want.

There is good news: you can control your presentation. You can change, modify, and otherwise improve your appearance.

Remember when you were a little kid and they told you, "You can't judge a book by its cover"? Then when you were older they said, "You only get one chance to make a first impression"? No wonder things like choosing the proper attire and hairstyle for a job interview seem so confusing.

Appearance counts in job searching. It would be a bald-faced, politically correct, touchy-feely lie to tell you anything else. Having said that, it's not as daunting as it sounds. Do you have to be the BEST looking to get a job?

Of course not.

Do you even have to be good-looking?

Not exactly.

So what the heck are you supposed to look like?

The goal in selecting your outfit and attending to your grooming for a job interview is to create a neutral, yet polished, physical appearance consistent with the type of job you are applying for, so that they notice and focus on you, your skills, your experience, and are not distracted by some specific of your appearance. You do not need to be gorgeous, a model, perfect, or thin to get a job. Nevertheless, you need to look neutral, and project a positive attitude. Enthusiastic. Friendly. Pleasant. *Normal.*

Remember, when an employer contacts you for an interview (assuming you applied via a résumé or application), they already believe that on paper you are qualified.

The purpose of an interview is to discover what you are like in person and to get an idea of your suitability for the position. Interviewers are primarily interested in two factors:

1. Can you do the job?
2. Will you fit in with the team?

"Fit in" means the interviewer can *picture you in their workplace*. As an average person, appropriately dressed, with nothing odd, off-putting, or distracting about you.

The interviewer will perform an instant assessment on both conscious and subconscious levels as whether you are someone he will want to have around every day, someone who can *get along with the rest of the team*.

It is brutally hard to look in a mirror and intentionally seek our own flaws. Nothing makes us feel as vulnerable as self-consciousness over our looks, especially considering the impact of that first impression.

A poor first impression at an interview can take you out of the running before you even have a chance to open your mouth.

Suggested Exercise: Analyze your own presentation.
How do you look? How do you feel? Check yourself and be brutally honest. If you are older, or overweight, short on funds, haven't had a decent haircut in years, chances are you feel bad, and feel trapped. Now relax, take a few deep breaths, and a good look at yourself in the mirror.

Let's start at the top. Specifically, your head and everything on it. The idea here is to look well groomed and *conservative*. People (by people I mean hiring managers and recruiters) have strong opinions when it comes to hair, and extreme or unusual hair can be an immediate disqualifier. A certain style might be your "thing," but is it really worth making yourself less employable?

• If you are serious about job searching, your hair should look clean and be conservatively styled.

• Get rid of the primary-colored streaks and the purple bangs. This is not junior high school, this is your life.

• For women, keep long hair off the face and contained neatly.

• For men with long hair, consider cutting off that

creepy old ponytail. Sorry to be the bearer of bad news, but long ponytails on men is a big turnoff to hiring managers and recruiters. They age you, for starters.

- If you are an older woman, update your hairstyle. If your hair is naturally gray, consider investing in a professional cut and color.
- I generally do not recommend men color their hair. For whatever reasons, it is always more noticeable as fake. However, if you insist, PLEASE get it colored at a salon.
- Men, please, no spiky, sticking-up hair. You should not look like you fussed over your hair before an interview.
- For men and women, a salon (or barber) is a good place to start your makeover. Stylists LOVE to help people. Just tell a hairstylist you need an update. They know what to do.
- If you need to and can possibly afford it, consider whitening your teeth. I know how expensive cosmetic improvements to teeth can be, but it is always worthwhile.
- For women, consider the combined effect of wearing glasses, a scarf, and earrings. Make sure it isn't too busy. Simplify. They want to see who you are.
- For men, make sure your eyebrows are not bushy to the point of distraction. If you have facial hair, a beard or goatee, make sure they are neatly trimmed. If you have a "soul patch," get rid of it.
- For men who choose to wear unusual beards, sideburns, or moustaches, you made that choice. Please understand that you are entitled to that choice, but an employer is entitled to select people he feels fit better

into his workplace.
- If you wear glasses, avoid anything that calls attention to itself. Those rectangular dark ugly squinty-eye frames that are still popular look good on NO ONE. Are you trying to get a job or impress an interviewer with your taste in eyewear?
- Don't hide behind heavy or outdated frames.
- Makeup should always be conservative. Less is more. Avoid brightly colored eye shadow and do not wear false eyelashes to a job interview, unless you are auditioning to be a Hooter's girl.

Now that you've planned your trip to the hair salon, let's move on. Consider all of your physical attributes below the neck. I know it's painful: analyzing your own body.

Other than poor hygiene or too much cologne, the immediate aspect an interviewer will notice is, of course, your size.

No employment professional will ever tell you this face-to-face, but the bigger you are, and I mean overweight or obese, the harder it will be for you to get a job.

If this is you, think about making positive changes concerning your diet and lifestyle. Please do not take it personally. Employers are concerned that you may not be able to stand on your feet for an entire shift, or that you will not be able to move quickly enough to assist in a preschool, or that you are not healthy enough yourself to care for a senior citizen.

You are an adult, and I suspect you already know if any of this applies to you.

It isn't all bad news, though. For many

administrative and other desk-bound positions, weight is usually not a factor for an otherwise excellent candidate.

If you are overweight but working on it, or happy with yourself as you are, immaculate grooming and a smiling, positive attitude will help keep an employer's focus on you and your skills.

Regardless of your size, choose properly fitted, professional clothes. Hiring managers expect you to look a certain way, even if the job you are applying for does not require professional business dress.

If you need financial help to afford business wear, there are many local and national organizations including Goodwill and Salvation Army thrift stores that carry reasonable priced, brand new with tags or gently worn professional clothing for men and women. Locate the resources in your own town. I've included several more in the list at the end of this book.

Interview Attire for Women
- A dark jacket and matching skirt (ALWAYS wear pantyhose if you are wearing a skirt), or pants.
- By jacket, I mean a professional suit jacket in a flattering style that fits well. Stick with standard suit fabrics only here, no tweeds, sweaters, or any unusual cut or color. Avoid wrinkle-prone fabrics like silk or linen. Black is your best bet; it's the universal interview outfit color.
- For skirts, wear a tailored, fitted knee or calf-length skirt. Avoid long flowing, flowery hippie skirts as interview attire.
- Pants can be trousers in a comfortable fabric. Please

do not wear leggings, yoga pants, or skin-tight stretch pants to an interview.
- Underneath the jacket, wear a collared blouse or scoop neck top, whichever you find more flattering, in a contrasting solid color.
- Leave off the scarf, unless you are interviewing for retail fashion. Scarves can make an outfit too "busy."
- Keep jewelry to a bare minimum. Do not wear dangly or jangly bracelets or earrings.
- NO talons. Keep your nails manicured and clean, but of moderate length. Long nails are a major turn-off to employers.
- Your purse should match your shoes, and be medium sized, not a huge tote bag bulging with stuff. Do not carry a backpack.
- Wear conservative closed-toed MODERATE heels or flats, or loafers if you are wearing trousers.
- Please do not wear those ridiculous too-high heels to a job interview, unless it is at Hooter's or a strip club.

Interview Attire for Men
- Wear a suit if possible.
- You can substitute a dark sport coat with matching or contrasting pants.
- Plain white or colored shirt with a matching tie.
- Make sure your shirt stays tucked in and that your pants fit in the waist.
- Wear a belt that matches your shoes. A solid leather belt, no braided or novelty belts.
- Polish your shoes.
- Do not wear aftershave or cologne.
- Clean under your fingernails.

- Make sure everything is clean and ironed.
- Carry a simple folder instead of a briefcase.

What Not to Wear on a Job Interview, EVER
- Flip-flops or sneakers.
- Visible undergarments (bras, bra straps, briefs, boxers), even if your bra straps match your top.
- Please. No visible *lack* of undergarments.
- Shorts or jeans unless you are specifically instructed to do so.
- Skirts too short.
- Pants too low-rise or too tight.
- Blouses that are too sheer, too low-cut or too short - don't show your cleavage or your belly.
- More on underwear and low-rise pants - make sure the top of your thong, if you wear one, doesn't show above your pants.
- No ridiculously high heels that make you teeter when you walk.
- A hat.
- A backpack. You don't need a briefcase, either.
- Sunglasses.
- Headphones or earbuds.
- There is an exception to the dress code: when you are given specific instructions on interview attire. If the hiring manager tells you to wear "khakis and a polo shirt," do *not* show up in a suit. They'll think you cannot follow simple instructions.

Speaking of first impressions, over fifty percent of employers now check Facebook, LinkedIn, and other social media accounts of job candidates.

Why? They want a glimpse into your life, and to see what you look like, of course. But they also search for warning signs you may *not* be the right candidate: inappropriateness, drama, semi-nude selfies, foul language, and all of those important things they cannot legally ask you in an interview. For example, how many children do you have? Are you an NRA member?

Are you revealing too much personal information on your Facebook page? On *other* Facebook pages? A snooping employer can easily uncover any comment you post on a public Facebook page, regardless of your own privacy settings.

Google yourself and see what comes up. You will be able to delete some of it, but not *all* of it. From now on, STOP commenting on all those Facebook pages.

If you have a LinkedIn profile, use a professional or business-like photo, and be sure your LinkedIn résumé matches the résumé you are sending to employers. Hiring managers and recruiters like to see LinkedIn profiles; it reinforces their belief that most people post only genuine information on LinkedIn. Besides, they might compare your profile with the information you provided to them when you applied.

Suggested Exercise: Clean up your social media.
Remove anything potentially harmful from your Facebook page, and learn to use your privacy settings. Your profile photo and cover photos are ALWAYS public. Use neutral, pleasant images. Remember, Facebook is forever.

Speaking of forever, any discussion of workplace

appearance must include tattoos.

Love them or hate them, tattoos are a *personal choice*. Like all personal choices, they come with consequences. As much as tattoos and piercings are about personal expression, as is your right, they are also equally about making a statement, one that can be perceived as intentionally in your face and anti-social.

Let's be honest about this. People are staring at your tattoos because you WANT them to. I have a tattoo, and mine could fit neatly into that category, except that my tattoo is not visible when I wear professional clothing.

You have the right to have tattoos. You also need to own that an employer has the right to his or her opinion, which may be that visible tattoos on employees are not part of their corporate culture. It would be hypocritical of you to claim an employer is judgmental for not allowing visible tattoos in their workplace.

Of course, some workplaces that are completely tattoo friendly. For those that aren't, consider investing in high-quality makeup designed to cover tattoos.

And piercings? Many employers cannot allow certain piercings for safety and hygiene reasons. Again, some simply *choose* not to allow them. It's your choice, too. Is it really worth sacrificing a nice administrative assistant gig with great pay just so you can wear those lip rings? I didn't think so.

CHAPTER 3
WHAT DO YOU WANT TO DO?

Me: "What kind of work are you looking for?"
Job Seeker: "Anything."
Well, congratulations. I *have* those jobs! Housekeeping, janitor, maid, kennel attendant, graveyard shift at the convenience store, they are always hiring. You can start tonight.

Now is that what you really meant? I didn't think so. By the way, some of those jobs, like residential maid services, can start at over $10 an hour and most of them are Monday through Friday day positions.

Magic Key: ALL jobs provide opportunities for growth.
You can learn new skills at any job and any age. We call these jobs— that are not your first choice—"stepping stone" jobs. Why are stepping stone jobs important?

Because it is easier to get a job when you already HAVE a job. Employers show a distinct preference for candidates that are already working, regardless of their current position.

How do you figure out what you *want* to do? Let's go back to that list you wrote in your notebook from Chapter 1.
- What are your goals?
- What is your dream career?
- What realistic jobs could you get that might lead to that career?
- Make a list of three things you can do *today* that will help move you in that direction.

Use this simple formula:
Where am I now?
Where do I want to be?
What can I do right now to help get me there?
If you answered these questions and came up with a solid goal, such as "nurse," the next step is to explore how to obtain the training you will need. If you came up empty on these, don't despair. Plenty of resources are available to help you figure it out, and you can start right at home.

The Occupational Information Network, or O-Net, is a website sponsored in part by the United States Department of Labor. It contains a wealth of detailed occupational descriptions and has a "My Next Move" section with an easy-to-use Interest Profiler.

Go to www.onetonline.org. On the right-hand side of the home page, look for the purple box that reads, "I want to be a…"

Click on it to get to the Interest Profiler, and simply

follow the directions.

Your best resource outside of the house is your local Workforce Center, Career Center, or CareerOneStop. These are state-run but federally mandated help centers for job seekers; see Chapter 5 for additional information.

Yours should be your *first* stop when you begin job searching.

Locate your closest center at www.careeronestop.org; all offer some version of a career exploration workshop.

Have you already decided that more education is the solution? Maybe you're considering returning to school to complete your high school diploma or GED.

In that case, go for it.

However, if you are thinking about a technical or trade school certificate, STOP and proceed with caution. First, do some research.

The Dark Side of Technical Schools: Things the Admissions Representative *Won't* Tell You

1. Your field is overcrowded with new graduates.

Let's use "medical assistant" as an example. I've picked that one because in certain regions, the field IS crammed with job seekers. Before you enroll in that pricey program (some are upwards of $17,000), ask the "admissions counselor" this: "How many medical assistants do you graduate each year?" Suppose they answer, "two hundred." Great, but that sounds like a lot of medical assistants. Are there *jobs* for two hundred brand new entry-level medical assistants in your area every year? Probably not, but it's likely that recruiter is going to tell you something different. Be *sure* you are not entering a field where the supply far exceeds the demand. Find out the truth yourself. Each region, county, and city is different.

You can find local labor market information on your state's employment department website, or at your local library. Learn for yourself, and do not be guided only by what the recruiter tells you. Remember, they get paid commission if they sign you up.

Another way to estimate if you'll have a job after getting $17,000 in debt is to study local job listings. Again, let's use medical assistant as an example. Check your local Craigslist postings, and the website "career" sections of hospitals, medical centers, and healthcare providers in your area. How many are hiring medical assistants? For those that are, read the job description carefully. How many employers want a year or more experience? Internships or externships generally do *not* count as experience.

Go a step further and call a few, and *ask* if they hire medical assistants *without* experience. I truly hope you'll be pleasantly surprised. In any case, you will gain valuable insight into whether a particular field is worth pursuing in your area.

2. You might not be a good fit for your chosen career, even if you graduate.

Just because you WANT to be a massage therapist,

CNA, medical assistant, or cosmetologist does *not* mean you will have the physical ability, interpersonal skills or aptitude to perform successfully. Most technical schools do *not* insist you undergo an assessment process before enrolling to ensure your suitability for a specific program and your future success in a chosen field.

They just take your money.

An admissions counselor or recruiter will not tell you that if you weigh three hundred and fifty pounds, your chances of success as a massage therapist are limited. Or that if you hate working with people, cosmetology isn't for you.

Be realistic, and get the facts about your dream job before committing to an expensive technical school. A massage therapist must stand on his or her feet eight hours a day, as well as projecting an image of health and fitness. A cosmetologist needs to have a keen sense of what a customer wants, and that means the ability to communicate with anyone.

3. We do not teach you the 'soft skills' vital for success in your new profession.

Bedside manner, compassion, kindness, empathy, patience, humor, understanding. All are skills vital to medical assistants, dental assistants, phlebotomists, and other healthcare providers, and almost never found in the curriculum of technical schools.

Does anyone WANT a medical assistant with an abrupt, cold personality? Of course not.

In the past, individuals were drawn to healthcare professions because they inherently possessed certain traits required for those jobs. Now, with technical schools promoting these careers as an instant way to become employable (for just $17,000), those eager to learn new skills lose sight of the real criteria needed to succeed in a medical setting.

You may be lucky enough to land a job after graduation, but deficiencies in the soft skills will quickly become apparent to an employer, and to your patients.

4. You might have some missing pieces that will prevent you from ever being hired in your new profession.

This one is hard to fathom, but true. Beware of enrolling in a school that insists, "You don't need a high school diploma or GED if you graduate from our school."

By the time you figure it out, you still need to pay back the $17,000.

Go back and complete your secondary education first.

A special warning if you have any kind of criminal history, even a misdemeanor: check your state laws before embarking on any formal education in the licensed health professions, childcare, or education. Find out if you are eligible to work in these professions with your history, if there is an exemption process that will allow you to work providing certain criteria are met, and if you will be eligible after a certain period of time has elapsed since your conviction.

Continuing education is just a part of becoming employed. Education is wonderful, but even a four-year degree does not automatically land you your dream job. You still need experience and work history.

Because chances are, even with that college degree, you are going to start in something other than your ideal job, or in a lower position than you anticipated, or part-time instead of full time. Again, these are "stepping stone" jobs. Part-time positions come with many benefits, including a lower-risk, less-pressure work situation in which to assess your family scheduling needs around your new employment.

If a quick fix is what you need, certain industries are always hiring. Telemarketing positions at call centers, companies that perform after-hours inventory in retail stores, preschool aides, in-home senior care, and direct care staff for developmentally disabled adults are all high-turnover occupations with plenty of job openings. Others in this category are hotel housekeeping, janitorial, cooks, and professional maid services.

"But I'm overqualified! And I need to make *at least* $25.00 per hour or it isn't worth it for me. Because that's what I *used* to make."

Were you a realtor? Mortgage specialist? A top-performing sales manager with decades of experience, earning six figures?

Here's my advice: Get over yourself, sooner rather than later.

First, because the economic climate has changed. Some of those jobs are, sadly, gone forever. Second, because it is imperative that you honestly confront the reasons you are not currently employed.

Your goal right now is to realign yourself with the world of work.

I can understand your bewilderment and frustration.

Remember money? Yes, me, too. I had one of those high-end jobs in an industry that is now gone. It's hard to accept that we are no longer "worth" what we made a mere few years ago. The truth is you may NEVER return to your previous income and status. Start somewhere, and start now.

You might have to climb back up that ladder one rung at a time. If you are home collecting $9.90 per hour in unemployment, or receiving even less in cash aid (welfare), you aren't even ON the ladder.

Please explain to me how a $12.00 per hour job is worse than collecting unemployment. Is it beneath you? You aren't working at all, remember? This might be your chance to take a job you *enjoy*. Love animals? Working with people? Go back and revisit all those job listings you noticed before and thought, "Gee, I'd love to do that, but it just doesn't pay enough. It's only two dollars an hour more than my unemployment."

Pick one, and apply for it. Get back on that ladder.

Magic Key: Volunteering
Regardless of what you want to be doing in the future, I can tell you the most important thing you should be doing right now if you are unemployed: Volunteering. Yes, that's right; I am telling you to work FREE. Why?

If you've been unemployed for a year, hanging out on your computer streaming Netflix all day, do you really need to ask?

The Benefits of Volunteering

1. YOU choose.
In the endless struggle that is job searching and all of its accompanying artificial emphasis on *someone else's* acceptance of *you*, volunteering gives you a chance to go where you are wanted or needed. Check websites such as Volunteermatch.org, or your local church or library. What's your passion? Animals? Seniors? What are your skills? Places like Habitat for Humanity always need willing and capable hands.
2. You can list it on your résumé just like a job.
There. Now you have current work experience, even if you've never worked or have been a stay-at-home mom and haven't worked in years.
3. You are networking and meeting people who can be potential employers or references.
4. It is a great way to gain skills or improve your English if needed.
5. Everybody can do *something*.
You can pack boxes at a food pantry, clean up after animals in a shelter, or stuff envelopes and answer phones to help raise funds.
6. It gets you off that couch and out into the world where you belong.
7. It feels good.
8. You can end up being hired. Remember how potential employers decide within a few seconds if you are a viable job candidate or not? Well, volunteering can sometimes mitigate that. Familiarity obscures barriers. Habits, quirks, and other things that detract from a great

first impression become invisible once someone gets used to you.

Suggested Exercise: Find three local places where you would like to volunteer.
Now call them for more information. The rest is up to you.

CHAPTER 4

JOB READINESS

No mystery here, "job readiness" is exactly what it sounds like: being physically and mentally prepared to abide by a set schedule every day that entails leaving the house, traveling to work, and performing successfully to earn an income while ensuring the needs of your household are met and the rest of your life is under control. As simple as it sounds, maybe your last job failed because you weren't ready to work, or did not have the necessary supports in place to succeed.

Suggested Exercise: Assess your own job readiness.
Write down your answers, "agree" or "disagree" with as much detail as you think necessary.

1. I am ready to connect with potential employers by filling out applications, or submitting a résumé in person or via email.
   - I have a résumé, or I have the information necessary to complete an application, including former

workplace addresses and phone numbers, the names of my previous supervisors, as well as former addresses where I've lived. Ten years' worth is the rule of thumb.

- I have the ability to use email.

2. I have the ability to communicate with potential employers by having accurate contact information like a working telephone number with a professional voice message. I do not let my voice mailbox get full. If contacting by email, I have the ability to check email at relevant intervals (once per day, NOT one per week).

3. Childcare, if necessary, is in place, and I know the days and hours I can and cannot work.

4. I have necessary transportation in place.

5. I have a criminal history but am ready and able to disclose it to an employer if necessary.

6. I do not have pending court dates.

7. I do not have major surgery scheduled.

8. I am not undergoing extensive medical treatment or recovering from injury or surgery.

9. I am not over seven months pregnant.

10. I am not in a rehabilitation facility.

11. My presentation is consistent with my stated job goals and I have enough appropriate clothing for work. For example, if you want to be an administrative assistant you know you can't wear overalls to work. You are aware of proper dress required for the position.

12. I am not involved in a pending worker's comp or disability case.

13. I have references with current contact information. I have contacted these references and received their consent to be contacted on my behalf.

14. I know what kind of jobs I am willing to do and capable of doing.

15. My social media (Facebook, Twitter, Instagram, and Linkedin) portrays me as a decent, normal person, with no drama or foul language. I do not have any potentially embarrassing photos that an employer might see, or my privacy controls are adequately preventing the public from seeing them.

16. I am not using drugs, including marijuana, even if I have a medical marijuana card. NEVER take a drug test you know you will not pass.

CHAPTER 5
THERE IS HELP FOR YOU

What if you've taken the self-assessment and it turns out not so great? You have a few pieces of the puzzle missing. Don't despair or beat yourself up. Focus on the resilience and life coping skills that got you this far in life. Use that to begin to build up your confidence. Channel your inner strength to work toward employment.

Start by locating the resources necessary to resolve some of your barriers. Typical barriers include:

Never worked
Homelessness
Convictions
Drug or alcohol dependence
Mental health issues
No childcare
No skills
No English
No high school diploma or GED

Where to Go for Help
Magic Key: American Job Centers
1. Your local Workforce Center, Career Center, or CareerOneStop. Though they operate under different names in different states, all are part of the American Job Centers network of resources.

To find yours, go to the www.careeronestop.org home page.

On the upper right-hand side, you will see a drop-down menu for State Job Banks.

Below that is a clickable link that reads: People + Places to Help. Click on it to find your closest center.

These local centers have a staff of full-time professionals trained and dedicated to assisting job seekers like you. Some states require you attend an orientation before using services; some do not. They offer résumé help, interview preparation classes, career exploration workshops, as well as employer panels and on-site Job Fairs or hiring events. They also are a repository for job leads, labor market information, and training options including on-the-job training. If you meet eligibility requirements (these vary from state to state), you may be assigned a case manager. A case manager is a professional counselor trained to provide an extra layer of individualized services based on your needs. This person also gets to know you, and can be a vital link between you and that job.

A Career Center can provide you with information on returning to school and completing your high school diploma or GED, which I strongly suggest you do, no matter what.

Some centers have re-entry programs for felons,

and offer assistance on attending clean slate clinics or refer you to specialized services.

2. Your local library.

Most libraries carry a variety of materials for job seekers including résumé help, post local job opportunities, and offer special programs such as basic computer classes.

3. Your county social services office.

If you are unemployed, struggling financially, and have a minor child or children, contact your county social services office. This agency can determine if you are eligible for temporary assistance in the form of a "welfare-to-work" program, and these can be lifesavers. Designed as a short-term safety net, these programs sometimes cover costs associated with transportation and childcare in conjunction with a commitment from you to obtain employment or continue your education. Once you embark on your new career, these supports may remain in place for a year or more. You must fulfill attendance and other requirements in these programs.

4. Your local mental health services agency.

If you have been referred to an agency and are receiving services for mental health issues or drug and alcohol treatment, remember that these organizations also offer a variety of job seeker resources. Many have wellness and stress management workshops, as well as case-managed job placement services.

5. Your local adult school.

The adult education center in your area may be a separate entity, or operate inside of your local community college or other learning center. Here you can enroll in courses such as high school diploma or GED, English, and basic computer skills.

6. Online.

The United States Department of Labor website, www.doleta.gov, offers a wealth of job seeker information, and special advice for recently laid off workers.

7. Your local church or human services organization.

Certain faith-based national organizations such as www.CatholicCharitiesUSA.org and www.ldsjobs.org (the Mormons) provide a wide range of free social services, including those for job seekers. The Goodwill is another national organization striving to help those with barriers become employed. Check online to find your local chapter.

8. Reentry programs.

If you have been incarcerated, there is an organization with branches in New York, Oklahoma, and California called www.CEOworks.org that provides help and training for felons in reentry. Your local Workforce Center, Catholic Charities, and Goodwill also help those with criminal histories.

CHAPTER 6

THE NUTS & BOLTS:
APPLICATIONS, RÉSUMÉS AND COVER LETTERS

Why do employers require applications and résumés? The short answer: to screen you out. In an earlier chapter, we talked about presentation. Presentation begins at the *first* point of contact, namely, the application or résumé. How you present on paper or in your online application is the first hurdle to successful employment.

Your goal is to get to meet them in person; their goal is to narrow the field. All other things being equal, an application is more important than a résumé. Remember, a key difference is that an application is a signed legal document, while a résumé is a snapshot of your skills and work history.

Applications
Again, a job application is often your first and maybe only chance to impress an employer. Even an online

application will reveal spelling and grammatical errors.

Before attempting to complete a job application, make sure you have all of the pertinent information in place. To recap, that means current contact info including a WORKING phone number with an acceptable voice message and no obnoxious music. Also, the names, addresses, and phone numbers of former employers including the names of your supervisors and your education history including where you attended high school. Include previous home addresses for the last ten years, and at least three professional or personal references with current contact information. Gathering this information can be difficult and time-consuming, but you only have to do it once. Just remember to keep it updated.

Note: References are gold. Ensure you have solid references with current contact information who will immediately respond to any potential employer.

Suggested Exercise. Create an application cheat sheet with all of your information in one place. Make it small enough (one sheet) to carry with you.

Some important things to know when filling out job applications in person:
- I can't say this strongly enough, but *dress as if you are about to be interviewed*. Even if, for example, you are shopping in a local store you like. You see a sign that reads, "Help Wanted." You are wearing sweats and no makeup. Do NOT give in to the temptation to ask for an application right there. You will blow your ONE chance

to make a good first impression. No matter how qualified you are, all they will remember is the sweats. Go home and change, then come back and ask for that application. Especially in a small, locally owned store where that person behind the cash register might be the owner.

- Neatness and completeness count. Fill out the application slowly and carefully. Take your time. If you bring it home, put it in a folder so it doesn't end up getting ruined or creased. Have your prepared information ready, and do not leave blanks.

- If you have had a series of short jobs recently, be sure you include them on your application. Why? Remember, this is a signed *legal* document. Those short jobs will magically appear if you make it to the background process. Don't cause confusion or make an employer think you are concealing facts.

- Make sure you are handing the neatly completed application to a hiring manager, not someone who might have a job-seeking cousin and will just toss your application in the trash the second you walk away. *Ask* for the hiring manager, and hand it to them. All you need to do is smile, say your name, and let them know you are applying for a position. Then thank them and walk away, unless they stop you. Again, be interview-ready when filling out applications in person.

- Go ALONE. Do not bring kids, friends, boyfriends, or family members.

- Do *not* use your phone as an address book or day planner. Sure, YOU know you're sitting there getting addresses and phone numbers off your phone. What it *looks* like is this: you are sitting there texting or Tweeting. With good reason, many employers are now restricting the use of personal cell phones at work. Texting at work is a habit employers hate.

Online Applications

There is a special form of hell reserved for job seekers: the online application. Online applications can be difficult, tedious, repetitive, and a test of your will and patience. Complete enough of these with no responses, and you start to feel like you no longer even exist. This is now the standard for many employers. Again, the process is much easier when you have all of your information readily available.

- Complete online applications with the same attention to detail (spelling, grammar, punctuation), as a paper application. At some point, many of these will end up printed out – and on paper.
- Read the position description carefully and include keywords from the description in your application.
- Complete it in one sitting. Even though there may not be a timed limit, many employers report tracking the amount of time an applicant spent completing an online application. Some report that they will "kick out" applicants who completed an application over a period of days, or logged in multiple times.
- Make sure you also have a résumé complete and in electronic form; many online applications ask for them.
- If you are planning to move and are applying online from out of town, bear in mind that some online systems are programmed to kick out out-of-town zip codes. In

fact, many employers report using a search function that eliminates candidates with addresses farther than a selected number of miles from the job location.

Online Assessments

Oh, what do they want, asking the same question nine different ways so you can work the graveyard shift in a WalMart warehouse? The answers are typically a closely guarded secret with the employers who use them. Why would they share? Then everyone could pass those nasty little tests.

A few tips for online assessments:

- In general, companies seem to favor answers that strongly agree or strongly disagree.
- Choose answers indicating that the manager or customer is always right.
- Show competitiveness.
- Answering "yes" to any form of this question will eliminate you immediately: "Have you ever taken anything from work, even if it was only a paper clip?"

The Trouble with Résumés

When you begin getting professional help with your job search, you will encounter tons of conflicting information. Much of it will be about résumés.

"Résumés are everything."

"Résumés are nothing."

Which is true? Both, of course. If you are applying to be an administrative assistant, for example, a résumé demonstrates that you possess the document formatting skills and business literacy required for the position.

However, if you are applying to be a home health aide, the employer needs to know your background, experience, and most important, what you are like *in person*.

The purpose of a résumé is to give the employer an instant picture of whether YOUR skills and experience match his job description, including the presentation and content of the résumé itself. That's it. Here's a recent gem from an employer:

"I don't really care about résumés, because truthfully, anyone can pay to have a great résumé. We know many people have résumés written by someone else. What I want to see is their ability to fill out an application, their personality, and some sense of what they would be like as an employee. That's why I'd rather have recruiting events and attend job fairs than screen résumés."

Another one, from a recruiter that hires hundreds of people each year, and spends countless hours at job fairs:

"Speaking, eye contact, appearance, handshake, attitude, and aptitude are what I look for. I've found great job candidates at hiring events whose résumés I would have thrown in the trash if I had not met them in person first."

In my professional opinion, the trend is slowly moving *away* from both résumés *and* online applications for specific industries, especially customer-facing hospitality and care giving positions, in favor of in-person applications, job fairs, and recruitment events. Employers filling positions where a positive attitude counts rarely find résumés useful in offering worthwhile insight into the personality of the job seeker.

An equal number of employers don't mind screening hundreds of résumés for each job filled, so you are going to need at least a simple one. If you have sufficiently addressed your job search readiness, now is the time to begin working on your résumé. This is where your local Workforce Center can help.

And here is where the trouble starts. A sharp, professionally written résumé can mislead hiring managers and recruiters.

How can this happen?

Many Workforce Centers and other job seeker services utilize online résumé-creating programs to help you create a résumé quickly from scratch. Careerbuilder's "RésuméHero" is one of these. They do provide nearly instant gratification in terms of creating your first résumé, but watch out:

- The software has built-in, pre-written descriptions of common job duties. Imagine you and three other individuals at your local Career Center are each creating a new résumé using the same online program. You have similar work experience, are looking for care giving jobs, and are all attending the same job fair. Unless you've taken the time to personalize those job duties, you could all end up with disturbingly similar résumés.

- They can exaggerate your actual literacy or English skills. Having an error-free résumé written in perfect English, if you do not speak perfect English, is going to surprise an interviewer— and not in a good way. It will even startle an employer calling you on the phone, because it appears deceptive. The résumé should *sound* like you wrote it. State that English is not your first language if you are not fluent.

- They use dumb "core competencies" as pseudo-skills. Again, "reading comprehension" and "active listening" are NOT real skills. They are social services jargon. Having faith that these mean anything to a hiring manager is false hope. "Cleaning" and "typing" are *real* skills.

So, what should you do? Ask for help with a simple résumé. Write it out by hand on a piece of paper before you start with a computer version. Know what you want it to express. Keep this in mind:

Hiring managers spend an average of ten seconds looking at a résumé. That covers just about the top 1/3 of the page.

The Objective
This is a much-debated subject among employment professionals. What *is* an objective (or goal, or summary), and do you need one on *your* résumé?

- It is a one-line statement of *why* you are submitting your résumé.
- You can customize it, make it generic, or leave it off.
- ***For my money, leave it off.*** A poorly worded objective can wreck your chances, especially if it has too much "I & my" language.
- Avoid "I" and "My," and never, ever make it about

YOU or YOUR "personal growth."

- Good Example: Seeking to provide excellent customer service in a team-oriented environment.
- Bad Example: I am seeking a customer service position where I can use my skills and experience to further my personal and professional growth.
- Don't accidentally leave an objective from an alternate version of your résumé for the wrong position.

Skills vs. Competencies

Online résumé programs often include "core competencies" as a résumé section. The available pre-written selections include nonsense like "analytical thinking" and "problem solving." Change the section title to "skills" instead. Even if you have little work history, avoid listing things like "active listening" and "reading comprehension" as skills.

Functional Résumés

What is a "functional" résumé? Social services folks (including places I've worked) seem to love these. However, they love them from a place of helping, an idealized, false world where a hiring manager has the time to THINK about each résumé and what it says about an applicant, instead of a thirty-second glance. Many employment professionals work only with job seekers, not hiring managers and recruiters. I work with hiring managers and recruiters.

News flash:

Ninety-nine percent of hiring managers and recruiters HATE FUNCTIONAL RÉSUMÉS.

A functional résumé lists specific *skills* as your selling point, and hides your job history way at the bottom of the page, including only the places you worked and dates. A functional résumé is designed to hide a spotty work history, or no recent employment.

Hiring managers and recruiters *know* this. Again, I'll stress the value of taking a volunteer position, even for two hours per week. You can stick THAT on your résumé, right under current employment.

Résumé Basics

- Start with your contact information at the top, and make sure it is current.
- Include city, state, and zip code. A résumé that only shows a name and phone number is going straight into the trash. Don't make employers guess or wonder where you live.
- Include a *professional* email address. No "partybabe10@aol" or "Dave420@hotmail." Employers know what "420" means.
- Leave lots of white space. Don't use big chunks of bunched-up words.
- NEVER lie or fudge on education or work history. They will find out. Don't use someone else's address if you don't actually live in the area in which you are job searching. That's otherwise known as "a lie."
- Check your spelling, grammar, and punctuation. Use your spell-check. Have someone else read it. Sloppy typos and lazy mistakes are a huge turn-off. Remember, this represents *you*. You know that the letter "i" is never written in lower case, right?

- Include a "skills" section with your hard-core skills like, Typing (50 wpm), CNC Operator, or Phlebotomy. You will tweak these keywords to match specific job descriptions.
- Start with your most recent job when listing work history. Include the MONTH and YEAR you started and left each job. Leaving off the month to obscure a short stint at a job is deceptive, and hiring managers will know it.
- Ten years is the rule of thumb for work history.
- Be careful using the words "I" and "my" if you include an objective.
- Never include references, personal information, or a photograph on a résumé.
- Do not write "References Available upon Request" on your résumé.
- Fancy résumé paper is no longer necessary; most employers end up scanning them into a database.

Top Résumé Tips from Recruiters
- A résumé should be an advertisement addressing the needs *of the potential employer*.
- Highlight achievements in bullet points instead of just listing duties.
- If you lack specific experience for a position share your GOALS instead. Include a few goals right under the objective – do research on the company and use those goals to state what *you* could bring to the position.
- Have one résumé for EACH job. Yes, customize your résumé for every job.

Suggested Exercise: Create your résumé.
I'm including a simple résumé format. Put your objective (if included), skills, and recent work history in the top 1/3 of the page. Why? Again, hiring managers and recruiters often get no further than this in their thirty-second scan of your résumé. This is the valuable real estate.

Does your résumé have to be one page? Of course not.

If you have extensive experience, one and one-quarter to one-half page is fine. But remember the thirty-second rule.

Simple Résumé Format

Name
Address
Phone, email

Objective
Make it a good one, or skip it.

Skills
- List *actual* skills, separated by commas: Typing, Hanging Drywall, 10-Key, Machinist, Customer Service.

Work History
- Most Recent Employer   Dates Employed

Job Title, Company, City and State
Brief bullet point list of duties or accomplishments

- Next Employer   Dates Employed

Job Title, Company, City and State
Brief bullet point list of duties or accomplishments

Education or Certifications
List school, city and state, and date.
If you are over fifty, leave off the dates.

The Cover Letter

This is about as much fun as doing your taxes, isn't it? Does anything make you squirm quite the same way as trying to compose a cover letter?

Some cover letter tips:

- Make it good or don't do it. A bad cover letter can kick you out, even with a good résumé.
- If you are an exceptional writer – go for it! Use your creativity to describe what you would bring to the position.
- Use a cover letter to highlight additional skills or experience – do not repeat things already on your résumé.
- Use it to explain gaps in employment or things that aren't apparent from your résumé, such as a career change.
- If you are applying for a job in another area, use it to clarify your status. For example, that if hired, you would "relocate immediately." NEVER use a local address (friend, relative) if you are applying from out of town.
- If you absolutely cannot find the name of a person to apply to, simply write "Hello" as the greeting. Do not use "To Whom it May Concern."

A simple, basic cover letter format

Greeting:
Dear [insert name of recruiter or human resources contact],
Body:
First paragraph: State the position you are applying for, and where you found it.

Middle paragraphs: State your specific qualifications for the position, tailored to the specific company, and in a way that is different from your résumé. This is the place to promote yourself, especially if you write well. Keep it brief. A cover letter should not be longer than one-half to two-thirds of a page.

Final paragraph: Discuss the next steps. Say that you look forward to hearing from them.

Provide your email address and phone number, and thank them for their time.
Close
Best,
[Insert your name]

CHAPTER 7

WHERE TO SEARCH FOR JOBS

You are finally ready, armed with your résumé, application materials, interview clothes, and all that other stuff we talked about. Now where do you find jobs?

Online

Online job searching is standard these days, but you should know:

- Pay attention to the posting date. Anything over a week old, unless there is a specific closing date, is useless. And a week is generous.
- Don't randomly apply for everything.
- Don't apply for multiple positions at a single company.
- DO NOT waste your time posting your résumé or otherwise "signing up" for any third-party job search sites to have them email you leads.
- Don't clutter your email inbox by subscribing to daily job listings.

- Do not pay for "upgrades," and do not apply for jobs through a third-party site. That includes Jobing.com, Bright.com, Indeed.com, and any of the numerous others.
- Do not even post your résumé on CareerBuilder. Less than 1.2% of employers use CareerBuilder to find candidates. You will get nothing but spam in your inbox.

I personally have *never* heard a single employer say they find candidates by searching third-party job sites. Third-party sites just gather your information and attempt to sell you things. You *can* use them to *find* a job posting. For example, you see an AT&T job posting on Indeed.com. Fine, now go *directly* to the AT&T website to apply.

Some common job search websites, in no particular order:

www.careerbuilder.com. Use the advanced search function to filter out national jobs. Make sure you are applying directly to the company website.

www.craigslist.com. Be careful, hidden among the real jobs are many scams. Use your head. If it sounds too go to be true, it is.

www.usajobs.com. Federal jobs in your area. This is a lengthy application process with many steps.

www.edjoin.org. This is a great job site. You can search by region to find all of the schools in your area. The jobs posted range from custodian to superintendent. Schools offer many high-end clerical and administrative positions, as well as simple things like "noon duty supervisor."

www.indeed.com. Be careful of applying through third-party sites, and note the number of days since the job was posted. Anything over seven days is probably a waste of time.

www.ejobs.org. This site, primarily for environmental jobs, has a state-by-state listing of government agencies and non-profits.

Don't forget to check your own local city and county websites for job postings, as well as utility companies, transit companies, hospitals, businesses, and local non-profits.

What about LinkedIn, Facebook, or other social media to find jobs?

Facebook in general is of limited value as far as job searching, though there are exceptions. For example, if you would like to work for a nearby business, follow their Facebook page to determine if they post jobs opening on it.

For unemployed professionals, having a LinkedIn page is a useful way to post your full résumé as well as creating visibility. Follow their tips and construct a profile that shows you at your best. Most posted positions on LinkedIn jobs are high-level professional and technical.

Job Fairs and Hiring Events

The most effective way to apply for a job is in person. Keep your eyes open for these opportunities. Check your local employment center, local news sites, the public library, and Craigslist for hiring events or job fairs where employers conduct on-the-spot interviews.

Obviously, face-to-face contact with potential employers is vital in getting hiring. Any situation that allows you to bypass those first steps designed to screen you out— the online application or résumé submission— is a golden opportunity.

Magic Key: Seek opportunities to meet employers in person.

How to Work a Job Fair

- A week before, prepare by finding out which companies will be there. Research the ones that interest you.
- Prioritize: you will not be able to talk to them all.
- Prepare specific questions for each employer.
- Make sure you have appropriate attire – dressing for a job fair is the same as dressing for an interview.
- On the event day, ARRIVE EARLY. Job fairs tend to be crowded.
- Go alone, or with a fellow job seeker. No kids, friends tagging along, or your mother.
- Be prepared to smile, shake hands, and ask meaningful questions.
- When you have positive interactions with recruiters, get their business cards. Promise to follow up.

- I'm going to go against common wisdom here and tell you not to concentrate on handing out résumés. First, so many people leave résumés that they often end up being tossed instead of carried back to the office. Second, employers are also known to scrawl first impressions on the back of your résumé. Like "loud," or "don't hire."
- Bring résumés, but only give them out if a recruiter asks for one.
- Listen to instructions. For example, if a recruiter tells you, "Go and fill out our online application then call me Tuesday morning," DO IT. On Tuesday. Not Monday. Not Wednesday.
- After the job fair, follow up as promised.

Jobs in Your Backyard
Find the job openings in your neighborhood, and apply in person. Google your home address. Now use the "search nearby" function and select a business category. You might be surprised at how many potential employers are within easy striking distance of your home. This is a good place to start if you have transportation issues; expanded Google search results show public transportation routes in some areas.

I know this is a scary idea, but you've prepared your application materials and polished your presentation. So go in person to select businesses. Managers are super-busy, especially in popular restaurants and retail stores. Hiring is a big drain on their time. Who wouldn't like the ideal candidate to walk in the door before the manager has time to write the job posting?

- Go in the morning, right at opening time.
- Ask to speak with the hiring manager.
- In person can also start with a phone call.

You: "May I speak to the hiring manager, please?"
Hiring Manager: "This is Joe, how may I help you?"
You: "My name is [your name]. I'm an excellent server (bartender, cashier, etc.) with five years' experience. Are you currently hiring?"
Hiring Manager: "As a matter of fact, we are. Can you come in this afternoon for an interview?"
You: "Of course!"

Networking
Allegedly, 87% of all jobs are found through networking. "Networking" isn't some mysterious business ritual; it simply means developing and using business or personal connections to gain access to decision makers at a company.

Start by determining your immediate sphere of influence (your informal network). This consists of family, friends, former employers, former co-workers, school, clients, customers, church, service providers (mechanic, doctor, dentist). Then let everyone know that you are job searching. You might be surprised by who knows whom.

From here, you can branch out and find local formal networking events.

Check your local city website as well as Chambers of Commerce for information on local business and networking events.

Suggested Exercise: Write down your personal network. Keep a log of new contacts you meet who can help connect you with a job.

The Personal Commercial

Preparation for networking events begins with developing a "personal commercial," also known as the Elevator Pitch. This is a thirty-second statement about who you are and what you can do for the employer. It is also useful when answering the interview question, "Tell me about yourself."

- Speak for thirty seconds, and then stop.
- Make it short, direct, and to the point.
- Give a clear idea of who you are, what you can do, and what you are looking for.
- Practice saying it aloud. Pay attention to how it sounds, and adjust anything that feels uncomfortable or awkward.

An example, "My name is Joe Smith. I'm a customer service professional with over ten years' experience in inbound and outbound calling. I've managed a call center with twenty direct reports and consistently exceeded sales quotas. I'm looking for full-time employment and the opportunity to make an impact driving sales for your firm."

Work-at-Home Jobs

If you have first-rate computer skills and a reliable computer (your 'smart phone' doesn't count), there is work you can do at home. Try Elance.com or Fiverr.com for data entry, typing, translating, research, formatting, and graphic arts jobs, but remember these are intensely competitive and no guarantee of steady income.

Care.com is a site that allows you to post a personal profile and offer services. These include in-home seniors and childcare, pet sitting, personal assistant, and similar work. This is worth exploring if you have a squeaky-clean background, are computer-savvy, and have experience in these fields. Again, no guarantee of steady income and you need to be communicative and reliable.

Recap: Applying for Jobs
- The best way to apply for a job is IN PERSON.
- Have a sense of urgency. If you find a listing that suits you, apply NOW. Don't think about it for a few days, or put it off. The shelf life of a job posting is short.
- Whenever you apply for a job, follow directions. Read the posting carefully. If they ask that you put the position name in the subject line of an email, do it. Follow requirements on "How to Apply" exactly as written.
- Don't ever ask to apply for "Anything." Be specific. "Anything" means you don't know anything about the company.
- Track your job search. Keep a detailed list. It doesn't have to be fancy. Just use your notebook. Number each job applied for, date applied, company name, and leave a little space between each. Cross off rejections, but leave them legible. Review your list daily while a job is still "hot" – the first two weeks after you

apply.

- Be ready for a phone call. Do NOT answer the phone while driving. It is okay to call them back.
- Know why they are calling you – refer to your job search record.
- Be RESPONSIVE. Check your voice messages and emails every single day when you are job searching. Return calls and emails immediately. They'll only call once, believe me.

Magic Key: The number one factor retail employers are looking for in a job applicant? Open availability.
This will get you responses faster than anything else will. Remember, retail is all about evenings and weekends. If you want to work at Macy's but can't accommodate retail hours, maybe you should consider a different type of work. No retail employer wants to hire someone who refuses to work weekends. Sorry, don't shoot the messenger.

CHAPTER 8

THE INTERVIEW

Oh. My. God. They called for an interview and you can't believe it. Your first reaction is joy, followed immediately by petrifying fear. Interviews are a big deal. It breaks down something like this: the average employer will scan 80-100 applications for a job. Another review will send 15-20 into the pre-interview round. Some hiring managers phone screen, some don't. An average of three to five will be interviewed. This varies, of course.

How do you prepare?
- Start researching the company immediately. Ideally, your research should begin when you *apply* for the job, not when you get the interview.
- If no salary was stated in the job posting, research the typical salary range for that position.
- Select and prepare your interview outfit using the guidelines discussed earlier.
- Practice interview questions.

- Consult your local Workforce Center to arrange a mock (pretend) interview with a professional.
- Find out where the interview is being held and if possible, do a test-run (travel to the site) to ensure you know where it is and can arrive on time (ten minutes early).
- And leave off the cologne or perfume. Trust me.
- Do not smoke before an interview.

Here is something I hope you take to heart if you arrive at an interview to find other candidates waiting: NEVER compare yourself to others.

Years ago, I happily went off to my first day at a new job, a position in which I was expected to have some authority. All seemed well until another new employee arrived at the orientation. She was a tall, sleek, impeccably dressed blonde wearing a luxurious camel hair coat over a perfect suit.

I was crestfallen – and immediately self-conscious. How *dare* she show up and be so good-looking? This goddess-like person would be reporting to *me*. Next to her, I would disappear, like a little brown mouse.

My hopes of corporate success were spoiled - by CEO Barbie.

Then something amazing happened. She spoke.

As I later described it: I was only intimidated until she opened her mouth. Yes, that's right. Miss CEO Barbie let fly with the by-gosh *dumbest* stream of chatter you ever did hear.

Bless her heart, I nearly felt sorry for the poor thing—and my self-confidence was magically restored.

The point is, no matter how slickly competent a rival *appears*, you have no idea what they have in their *head*.

How to Maximize that First Impression

Well, you *look* great because you got a nice haircut and found some choice interview clothes at the resale store.

You practiced interview questions with an employment professional or a friend, and have answers and questions ready.

You researched the company and position, and are prepared.

You know where you are going, and how long it will take to get there.

You are calm, but enthusiastic, pleased to be interviewed, and your smile and attitude reflect that. You have everything you need and head to the interview location.

- Time counts: unless instructed otherwise, arrive seven to ten minutes early. Anything longer makes you seem desperate or unable to manage time. And late? Don't even go there. However, if you've done everything possible and something out of your control makes you late, call if you can to let them know. Then own it and apologize when you do arrive.
- If you are unexpectedly sick with a bad, sniffly, sneezy, snot-oozing head cold, it is okay to call and ask to reschedule.
- Remember that the interview begins the second you pull into the parking lot. Tip: Wash your car.
- Assume you are being watched. Hiring is a big deal,

and everyone is excited to get a look at the candidates. Remember, while you're screaming at your boyfriend on your cell phone in the parking lot, even in your car, you may be visible or worse, audible.
- Do not bring a drink in with you.
- Do not chew gum.
- Do not bring another person with you.
- **Before you go inside, put away that cell phone.** Listen, I'm telling you again, the receptionist and everyone else are watching you. Do *not* keep your application cheat sheet on your cell phone. Sitting there scrolling through your contacts does not make you look tech-savvy, it makes you look like you are Tweeting or Facebooking. Keep that information on a sheet of paper in the nice folder or portfolio you are carrying. That is ALL you should be carrying.
- Again, NO CELL PHONES. Turn it off. Put it away. Leave it in the car.
- **And NO iPAD!** You'll look like a jerk waving that thing around.

Be Nice to the Gatekeeper
Yes, the receptionist. She now holds the power of life or death over you. Any sour faces, eye rolling, impatience, or other uncivil behavior will be promptly reported immediately after (if not BEFORE) you even meet the hiring manager.

Sit vs. Stand?
Some employment professionals believe it is better to stand than remain seated while waiting to be

interviewed. I say NO. Why?
- It is easier to conceal nervousness when seated.
- You cannot relax while standing.
- Standing looks weird and impatient.
- You will irritate the gatekeeper (that all-powerful receptionist).

Instead, pay attention, and stand when you see your interviewer approaching. This is the moment you've prepared for: the first impression. You are going to *shine* in that first few seconds. You stand quickly and smoothly, smile, make eye contact, and introduce yourself, extending your hand.

How to Shake Hands

Grip FIRMLY. The web between your thumb and forefinger should connect with the same spot on the interviewer's hand, and then give one pump, two pump, and release. Got that? Practice.

Firm grip, web to web, one pump, two pump, and release.
- Do not bone-crunch.
- Grip firmly, even if the interviewer's grip is weak.
- No limp, fishy handshake.
- No "lightly by the fingertips."

From here, simply follow the interviewer's lead.
- Wait until you are invited before you sit.
- For women, place your purse at the side of the chair, by your feet. Don't clutch it against your chest.
- Do NOT take notes. Taking notes is distracting and

worse, disengages that all-important eye contact. Whoever thought taking notes at an interview was a GOOD idea? Is the interviewer supposed to pause until you are done scribbling? Just don't do it. It is bad advice.
- Now relax. Everything is going to be fine.
- Again, they invited you to the interview because they already believe you are qualified for the job.

Typical Interview Questions
Many online and Workforce Center resources are available to expand on the general ideas here.

Q. Tell me about yourself.
A. This is where to use that personal commercial discussed in an earlier chapter. Speak for thirty to sixty seconds, then shut up and wait for the next questions.

Q. What interested you about this job?
A. This is where your research pays off. Frame your answer to indicate that your career goals meet the requirements of the position.

Q. What do you know about this position?
A. You had better be able to answer this one.

Q. Tell me about your strengths.
A. This is a good one to research. Think about the key responsibilities of the position you are interviewing for and relate your personal characteristics to it. "I'm flexible" could be a strength in a position that requires you to wear many hats. This is a far easier question than

its evil twin, "Tell me about your weaknesses."

Q. Tell me about your weaknesses.
A. A ton of job search literature has been written on this one question. Obviously, blurting out "I'm always late but working on it," is a huge mistake. Yes, it is a trick question. They do not actually want you to have any weaknesses, much less admit to them. And they've all heard the "I'm too much of a perfectionist," line before. The key is to make it authentic to *you*, and to make it something that will not eliminate you from contention. For example, if you are interviewing for a file clerk position that requires no computer skills, it is okay to say, "I would like to develop my Excel skills."

Q. Describe a time when you disagreed with your supervisor. How did you resolve the problem?
A. A good answer here is something along the lines of, "I've learned to professionally disagree, but always adhere to company policy." Or, "I find that keeping the lines of communication open helps to prevent this kind of situation in the first place."

Typical Situational or Behavioral Questions
Q. Describe a time when you worked as part of a team. What did you do to ensure the team completed the goal?
A. Have a prepared story for several of these instances.

Q. Describe a time when you dealt with a difficult customer. What did you do to ensure the customer went away satisfied?

Magic Key: Any customer service question involving an angry customer should start with you reassuring the customer that their concerns are being heard.

Top Interview Tips
- Prepare your thirty-second commercial to answer the "tell me about yourself" question.
- Research the company so well that you can state, "I want to do (fill in the blanks) for you." For example, "I want to provide excellent customer service for you."
- Prepare questions based on your research.
- Never be negative!
- Bring copies of your résumé in a portfolio or decent quality folder.
- When the interviewer asks, "do you have any questions for me?" A "no" answer will usually eliminate you as a job candidate. It means you just didn't care enough to find out anything about the company or the position. I wouldn't hire you, either. So do your research.

What to Ask
- What is a typical day like in this position?
- If I joined your team, what current projects would I be involved with?
- What are typically the biggest challenges of this position?
- Why is this position open?
- What do YOU like about working here?
- Who else has been successful in this job? What type of person?

- What qualities are you looking for in the ideal candidate?

Magic Key: RESEARCH the company. Ask intelligent questions and know WHY you want to work there. Most important, know what YOU can do for THEM.

What NOT to Say
- What would I be doing?
- What are the benefits?
- I'm nervous.
- Nothing is more important to me than my kids and family.
- How much does this position pay?

You should already have some idea of salary going into the interview, based on your research and preparation. But what if the question does come up, "What is your starting salary range?"

Unless you have an absolute drop-dead minimum, you should answer, "Whatever is typical for a candidate with my skills and experience."

Ending the Interview
- Be sure you ask the next steps, what to expect if you are to be moved along in the process. What is the time frame? How will they contact you?
- End where you started, with a handshake and a smile.
- Remember to ask for a business card.

- As you are leaving, remember you are still "on stage." Eyes will be on you until you are out of the building, and out of the parking lot.

After the Interview
- Send a thank-you note. An email is fine, but an actual hand-written note is better.
- If they said to "call if you haven't heard from us in a week," call in a week. NOT two days. If they say THEY will call in a week, give it eight days before YOU call THEM.
- Then, take their lead. Do not keep calling if they say, "we will call you."
- Don't stalk them. Never call and then hang up when voice mail picks up.
- For years, common job seeking wisdom advised candidates to "be aggressive," in post-interview follow-ups. Do not make repeated unanswered contacts to an employer after an interview. Believe me; they will not perceive you as a "go-getter." Try "nut" instead.
- Put your energy and frustration into applying for the next job, and write it off to experience.

Here is a harsh truth: the hiring process can be poky, frustrating, and seemingly moving at a glacial pace. However, an interview is a lot like a first date: if they *really* want you, you will know it sooner rather than later. If they don't call, as the saying goes, they are just not that into you. Move on.

After the interview, IMMEDIATELY write down any impressions of your performance. Ask these questions and rate yourself however works for you:

- Was I prepared by being dressed appropriately, arriving on time (ten minutes early), and in a relaxed, calm frame of mind?
- Did I shake hands firmly, smile, make good eye contact, and wait to be asked before I sat?
- Was I friendly, upbeat, and enthusiastic about the position?
- Did I speak clearly, at a comfortable rate, and not say "um" or "like"? Older people especially hate hearing "like" as every other word.
- Did I maintain appropriate facial expressions?
- Did I relate former work experience to the position without speaking negatively of my former employer?
- Did I focus on my personal strengths, skills, and accomplishments, with prepared stories to illustrate each?
- Did I listen to the questions and pause to think before answering and without interrupting?
- Did I talk too much?
- Did I omit any personal drama and not say things like "I really need a job?"
- Did I ask questions that indicated I researched the company and position thoroughly?
- Did I ask for the job and clarify the next steps and timeframe?
- Did I get the interviewer's name and send a thank you note?

Suggested Exercise. Make a post-interview assessment cheat sheet. Use it.

Alternative Interview Methods
The phone interview.
- Have your résumé in front of you and be in a quiet place where the kids or pets will not make noise in the background.
- Do not answer the phone while driving.
- Do not say, "Hello?" as if you were not expecting a call. Say, "This is Mary Smith (insert your own name)."

The group interview.
These can take many forms, but the basic premise is that a group of candidates will be questioned one at a time in the same room, or asked to role-play.
- Be friendly and outgoing.
- Listen carefully to instructions.
- Do not compare yourself to others.

The panel interview.
You alone, in front of a group of interviewers. These can be unnerving, to say the least.
- Keep calm and don't fidget.
- As you answer the questions you, make eye contact with each member of the panel.
- Focus on the questions and answers, not how you believe they are responding to you: there could be a little bit of "good cop, bad cop," going on. This means at least one member is intentionally being rude in an attempt to see how easily you are rattled.

Second Interviews

Ugh. If there is anything even more ridiculously unnatural than an interview, it is the dreaded SECOND interview. Or as I call it, "A bunch of people who can't make up their bleeping minds." Second interviews fly in the face of all that wisdom on the importance of first impressions, don't they? If you find yourself in this position, prepare as you did for the first interview, but ask *them* what to expect.

Warning: if you've gone through several interviews at the same company and they finally say, "Can you just come back and meet with Chuck (or whoever)? He likes to meet all the new hires." Never assume this is just a formality and that you are hired. Believe me when I say that if someone is bothering to interview you, that person will also get to vote on whether you are hired.

How to Tell When an Interview is Going Well

Be wary of determining anything based solely on the demeanor of your interviewer. The fact that they are "nice" doesn't mean anything. They are professional. What are some real things to look for?

- The interview lasted a long time. Longer is better. Interviewers take more time with candidates they are interested in hiring. Unless *you* are doing all the talking, of course.
- They ask, "If we offer you the position, how soon could you start?" This is not a random, throwaway question they would ask someone who is not in the running for the position.
- They check your references. This is usually a sign you will be offered the position.

No Offers

The bad news is, you haven't had a job offer. But the GOOD news is, if you are getting interviews, so you're doing something right.

Here is a list of things interviewers will NEVER tell you:

- You were too nervous and fidgety.
- You had a limp fishy handshake, or shook too forcefully.
- You were inappropriately dressed for the interview (sloppy, flashy, sexy, casual, outdated, soiled).
- There was a big disconnect between the image of you they perceived via your application or résumé, and the person that showed up for the interview.
- You talked too much, interrupted, or used foul language.
- You commented on inappropriate topics when answering interview questions, and mentioned taboo topics like politics or religion.
- Your physical appearance was unpleasant (disheveled, bad hygiene, body odor, too heavy, too much perfume or cologne).
- Your eyes darted around during the interview or you looked down into your purse and obviously checked your cell phone.
- You stumbled over words (um, um) or repeat yourself, "like."
- You were pushy, aggressive, arrogant, a wise-ass, dull, loud, air-headed, or obnoxious.
- You fell out in the background check. They usually

will tell you if you've failed a drug test.

A list of gentle ways to check the above:
- Check your attitude. Make sure you breathe deeply and generate energy and enthusiasm in interviews. Be friendly and smile. Faking it is okay.
- Be aware of your body control. Center yourself and relax. Don't shake your leg or swivel in your chair. Pretend you are confidant and you will appear confidant.
- Listen to the questions and pause before you answer. Practice your answers ahead of time.
- In spite of everything, are you still letting little nasties about your former employers slip in? Are you talking too much about your kids? Your drama? Your hardships? DON'T. Employers do not want to help YOU. They want YOU to help THEM.
- When they ask, "Where do you see yourself in five years?" that means they are looking for long-term team members. This is good. Make sure your express your goals of growing within a company clearly.
- Do not be negative, ever.
- Again, NEVER take a drug test you know you will fail.
- Ask employers for feedback. This takes nerves of steel. And guts.

Ask yourself this: Do I really want to work? I know you completed the job readiness assessment, but just double check.

Are others (partner, family) discouraging you from seeking employment? Seek help from social services if necessary.

If you have a background, are you disclosing it on the job application? Nothing will kill you faster in a hiring process than surprises in your background – after you've signed an application stating there is none.

The Other Side of the Interview
It can be devastating, but it happens. You get to the interview, and realize that you don't want to work there. It can happen before you even sit down. You feel awful, may second-guess yourself, or question your own motives. If you feel the slightest bit uncomfortable, pay attention to your surroundings at an interview to figure out why.

You know that movie line, "Life is like a box of chocolates - you never know what you'll get"?

I hate that line.

What about the boxes that have diagrams inside the lid? You've all seen those. A diagram showing exactly which flavor is in which slot, designed so you don't accidentally sink your teeth into coconut when what you wanted was cherry.

Well, a workplace is like that, too.

You never know what you'll get – unless you pay attention for the clues and signals that serve as your diagram.

Remember, you are at an interview because of what YOU have to offer THEM, not vice-versa. Having said that, the job has to be a match. Here are some things to look out for so you end up with the hazelnut instead of that icky nougat.

Some interview red flags for the job seeker:

- The interview is in a weird place at a strange time. Like the back room of a half-finished warehouse at 7:30 at night. I'm not implying anything sinister; you can certainly get calls in the evening and interview on weekends. Most standard businesses keep standard hours, and have actual offices associated with them. If it looks shady, chances are it IS shady.

- The interviewer is late, and forgot you were coming. I am asked this all the time: "How long should I wait if the interviewer is running late?" That depends. If the receptionist is right on it and can say, "She just called and will be here in fifteen minutes and is terribly sorry," fine. Or if the time was misunderstood, and not by you. Knowing what I know now, if you get the slightest indication that they *forgot* you were scheduled, bail and don't look back.

- Anything that smacks of dysfunction. If you arrive and the place seems chaotic, it probably *is* chaotic. If the interviewer sits down and says "How soon can you start? We just had someone else quit," run like hell. This is not an opportunity. This is a warning.

- Employees complain about the place right in front of you. Worse, they approach you and say, "You don't want to work here." Again, a warning. Listen to them.

Pay attention to anything that "tugs" at your instincts.

Chapter 9

Hired – Accepting, Starting, and Keeping That Job

Understanding a Job Offer
You did it! You have a job offer. Well, congratulations!

But your work isn't over yet.

Here are some things to make sure you know BEFORE accepting, and listen carefully to ensure there is no miscommunication.

- Your schedule, including days, hours, and starting and ending times. Find out if this is a set schedule, or a changing schedule.
- Your work location. Is it always the same location?
- Your starting pay, and if benefits are offered. How long before you are eligible for benefits?
- Your expected attire.
- Is there training, and if so, how long? Is it paid training?
- What is the performance review policy?

Obviously, accepting a job offer is up to you; if all of the above are agreeable, you accept the offer.

At this point, you are not quite hired yet. Typically, you will now move to the background check and drug test process.

Again, never take a drug test you know you will fail.

Assuming all goes well in your background and drug test, you will be given a start date.

Before your first day, you need to know:
- Whom do you call in case of emergency and who is your boss?
- Starting date, time, and location, and to whom you report.
- Parking and other details. Do you check in at security?
- What documents do you need?
- When and how do you receive your first paycheck? What pay period is covered? Is the check mailed or hand-delivered?
- Is there a lunchroom? Anything else you need to know?

Before that first day, double-check all of the supports that will help you succeed.

Transportation – can you get there? Do you know alternate routes in case of a problem?

Childcare – is it in place?

A new job changes the dynamic between you and your significant other. Before you start a new job, sit down and discuss what you going to work will change in your lives. For example, who is responsible for household chores? Does someone else need to start dinner? Pick up the kids? Iron out all the little details that will help ensure a smooth transition back into your work life.

New Job Jitters – or a Horrible Mistake?
The first few days on a new job are always stressful. But what if something seems *really* wrong? Is there ever a good reason to quit a new job right away?

Listen, if you did your research properly and used your best judgment in paying attention to interview red flags and everything else we talked about in the "box of chocolates" discussion, you can avoid situations like this.

If you did ignore red flags, and find yourself in a bad situation, what should you do? How do you know what constitutes a bad situation?

These are some extreme instances where leaving a new job quickly is probably an option.
- You arrive for your first day and are assigned tasks that differ *in the extreme* from your stated job description, and were not discussed during the hiring process. For example (another true story), you were hired as a compounding pharmacy technician and they have you cleaning toilets in the employee cafeteria instead.
- You arrive at work the first day and are told that the first days (or weeks) will be "unpaid training," and this was not spelled out before.

- The agreed-upon work location changes unexpectedly and dramatically. For example, you were hired for the location two blocks from your house, and on the second day, they reassign you to a location forty miles from your house.
- There are obvious concerns for your physical safety, or conditions are sub-standard. For example, there are live electrical wires and ongoing construction in the hallways, or you have to go to the coffee shop next door to use the restroom.

If you've done your homework and paid attention, you will recognize any red flags long before you end up in this type of situation. Be aware that if this happens to you more than once, the problem is most likely YOU.

How to Succeed at a New Job

A job is a relationship. It takes nurturing, patience, communication, and understanding, just like all of our other relationships.

Every new job is traumatic in a way, but the fact remains, you cannot tell if you will like a job in just one week.

Our perceptions of a new workplace readjust themselves almost hour by hour in the first month on a new job. Things can change rapidly.

Make a commitment to yourself to keep an open mind, take each day as it comes, and to do your best.

Again, I hate to point fingers, but if you've left two or three jobs in six months that weren't temp jobs, reassess your desire to work, and your own job readiness.

Fitting In

You've probably heard the phrase "work culture."

A workplace "culture" is all of the unspoken things that are accepted as the standard way to behave in a specific organization. Every workplace has its own culture. Do they wear jeans, or business casual? Are people friendly, or professional and matter-of-fact at all times? Do the others all eat in the lunchroom? Does everyone arrive fifteen minutes early, or stay ten extra minutes?

In order to succeed, you have to do more than just your job. You have to become part of the team. Learn the culture. This is where "monkey see, monkey do" comes in handy.

- When you first start, watch and learn. Listen more than you talk.
- Pay attention to things like the dress code policy, tardiness, and lunch breaks. Stick to them.
- Do NOT over share about your personal drama, kids, errant boyfriend or baby daddy. Just don't. The less they know about your crap, the better. Don't let anything you disclose put you in a bad light. Husband in prison? Shut up about it. Your kids are on drugs? Again – silence is golden.

Save the Drama

In an ideal world, work is like an extended family: when things go wrong, they care about you. This is the reality of businesses: they exist to make money.

HOWEVER, employers hate drama. They do and don't care about your illness, family problems, and emergencies.

Successful adults manage their work lives. They don't take an extra day off when they could just as easily come to work after an illness or family crisis. They reasonably assess whether conditions at home or personal health are under control. Your employer hired you because he needs you; every unplanned day off someone takes will affect the whole business.

If this does not make sense to you, or is unacceptable to you, you may need to reassess your job readiness.

Tips on Staying Employed
- Be on time, every day. When you first start, you are being watched every second. Late three times in the first two weeks and guess what? You're fired. Lateness is the fastest way to wash out of a new job in an instant. Being on time also applies to all aspects of work including meetings, trainings, conference calls, appointments, lunch, and breaks.
- Develop your "soft skills." As mentioned before, these are the interpersonal skills crucial to workplace success. Communication, integrity, ethical behavior, politeness, and friendliness are just a few of these.
- Eat lunch in the lunchroom. Bring your lunch. This is a good place to find out insider information on office etiquette. Hang out. Don't scurry out to lunch alone every day your first week.
- Never, ever just not show up. Again, get your supervisor's contact information your first day. Find out whom to call if there is a problem. ALWAYS CALL if

you are running late, but if you make running late a habit, it will cost you your job.

- Have a backup plan for emergencies. If your child gets the sniffles at daycare, things like that. Then have a backup plan for the backup plan.
- Don't make a habit of assuming you can leave work at the drop of a hat for minor things.
- Be friendly, but do not take part in the office gossip.
- Be professional. Stay OFF your cell phone.
- Do NOT Facebook with your new co-workers. Do not post about your job on social media.
- Be busy, busy, busy. Find new ways to be useful. If you find yourself with free time, ask your boss for things to do.
- Be a Team Player. Accept duties not in your original job description (there are exceptions, as noted previously). Employers are trying to "do more with less" these days, and employees often have to wear many hats. "That's not my job," are the worst four words you can utter at a new workplace. Or old workplace, for that matter. Good employees co-operate and are team players.
- Pay attention to detail and take pride in where you work. If someone misses the trashcan with that candy bar wrapper, pick it up and throw it away.
- Make coffee in the lunchroom, get copier paper, do whatever little tasks you see others doing on a daily basis.
- Volunteer to help others.
- Be savvy. Be aware that if you work in a field where confidential information is exchanged, or your

company has a "trade secret," part of your responsibility as an employee is to guard this information carefully. Not everything that goes on at work is fodder for gossip with your friends, family, or spouse.

- Step it up. Arrive ten minutes early and settle in before the workday. This gives you a calm platform on which to begin your day. Whenever you can, offer to extend yourself. Work overtime, substitute for someone in a crisis, in other words: be flexible and go with the flow.
- Settle in. I have mixed feelings about this, but after your probationary period is up, personalize your workspace as much as is allowed.
- Be positive!

Chapter 10

Over Fifty but Under Sixty-Five

A gentle reminder to all of you job seeking in this age group: you still count. By this time, you've no doubt fought and won many battles in your life. You WILL make it through.

If you are newly separated from a job and not yet retirement age, the important thing is to stay connected. Seek whatever social and spiritual resources are available to you near where you live. Church, AA, NA, your local Workforce Center or Career Center. Stay around people. Try Meetup.com.

If I could give you just one piece of advice, it would be this: take another job as soon as possible, even if it is below your previous salary and expectations. Do something you enjoy, but stay in the game.

They say misery loves company, and that is especially true on the internet. It can help to read the stories of other people just like you, but negativity is infectious.

Seek solace instead. Your spirit has been broken, and you need to mend.

What you should be doing online is to create at least some social media presence. Ensure your Facebook page portrays what you would like employers to see. Follow the same general rules.

You can "brand" yourself effectively on Facebook if you are over fifty by displaying photos that show you as active and in-tune.

Biking, hiking, walking your dog, anything that suggests motion is good.

You should have a LinkedIn profile, with a professional photograph and a résumé that matches the résumé you send employers. Here, too, you can "follow" professional organizations that enhance your skills and experience.

There are certain jobs, as I pointed out earlier, that are always available. Some of these are human services jobs, and can be remarkably rewarding. If you live near organizations that provide services for developmentally disabled adults, they are usually looking for paid helpers, sometimes called counselors or community support facilitators that help these adults live independent lives. It doesn't require experience, just the desire to help.

So, what else do you need to do?
- If you are newly unemployed, again, get back in the game as soon as possible. The longer you stay out of the workforce, the harder it is to go back. You lose hope,

lose energy, and lose the *habit* of working.

- Tweak your résumé. If you refer to the simple format I included earlier, remember that ten years employment history is the rule of thumb. And remove dates of graduation from your education.
- Update your skills. Take computer classes if necessary at your local adult education or community college.
- Learn to type – or take a refresher course. Funny how typing is still a valuable skill. If you can type 60 WPM and have a typing certificate obtained in person from a staffing agency or adult school, you will be more employable.
- Update your look. As discussed earlier, little changes can make a big difference.
- Volunteer.
- Think outside the box. Do something you REALLY enjoy, even it is for ten or eleven dollars an hour and you used to make twenty-five.
- Be honest with yourself. Are you truly accepting of a new opportunity, or are you stuck with that mindset that you will be able to return to your earlier income level? Chances are you will not.
- Shake off the anger. Anger makes us bristly, blaming, and unemployable.
- Seek joy and peace in your family, loved ones, and even your beloved pets.
- Smile.
- Keep fighting.

LIST OF JOB SEEKER RESOURCES

The United States Department of Labor website offers a host of resources if you are laid off:
http://www.doleta.gov

Goodwill has a presence throughout the U.S. Many of their locations offer employment services and training programs, and they hire, too.
http://www.goodwill.org

You do not have to be a member of these religions to utilize their resources!

Catholic Charities offers different services in different locations, everything from housing and literacy to employment services.
http://www.catholiccharitiesusa.org/find-help

The Mormons also have a nationwide network of employment service resources.

http://www.ldsjobs.org

The Assistance League provides a wealth of volunteer opportunities around the country.
http://www.assistanceleague.org

The Ways to Work program provides low-interest loans, financial education, and support to families with challenging credit histories to buy expensive necessities such as a car for work.
http://www.waystowork.org

Modest Needs in a web-based charity providing one-time grants for those in need. Supports a broad range of needs on a case-by-case basis.
http://www.modestneeds.org

These two organizations operate in major cities around the country to provide professional wardrobes to men and women re-entering the workforce:
http://www.dressforsuccess.org
http://www.careergear.org

Support for those in reentry after incarceration:
http://jailstojobs.org

Reentry support if you live in New York, Oklahoma, or California:
http://www.CEOworks.org

State Resources
http://www.careeronestop.org

Check your state employment website for information on unemployment benefits, housing, health care, job search, training and education, and career information:

Alabama
http://www.joblink.alabama.gov

Alaska
http://www.jobs.state.ak.us/

Arizona
http://www.azjobconnection.gov

Arkansas
http://www.arjoblink.arkansas.gov

California
http://www.caljobs.ca.gov

Colorado
http://www.connectingcolorado.com/

Connecticut
http://connecticut.us.jobs/

Delaware
http://www.joblink.delaware.gov

Florida

http://www.employflorida.com

Georgia
http://www.dol.state.ga.us/

Hawaii
http://www.hirenethawaii.com

Idaho
http://labor.idaho.gov/

Illinois
http://www.illinoisjoblink.illinois.gov

Indiana
http://www.indianacareerconnect.com

Iowa
http://www1.iowajobs.org

Kansas
http://www.kansasworks.com

Kentucky
http://www.oet.ky.go

Louisiana
http://www.ldol.state.la.us/

Maine
http://www.maine.gov/portal/employment

Maryland
http://www.dllr.state.md.us/county

Massachusetts
http://www.web.detma.org/JobQuest

Michigan
http://www.mitalent.org

Minnesota
http://www.minnesotaworks.net

Mississippi
http://www.mdes.ms.gov/i-need-a-job

Missouri
http://jobs.mo.gov/

Montana
https://jobs.mt.gov/jobs/login.seek

Nebraska
https://neworks.nebraska.gov

Nevada
http://www.nevadajobconnect.com/

New Hampshire
https://nhworksjobmatch.nhes.nh.gov/

New Jersey
http://jobs4jersey.com/

New Mexico
http://www.jobs.state.nm.us

New York
http://www.americasjobexchange.com/NY/state-jobs

North Carolina
https://www.ncesc1.com

North Dakota
http://www.jobsnd.com/

Ohio
https://ohiomeansjobs.com

Oklahoma
https://servicelink.oesc.state.ok.us

Oregon
http://www.worksourceoregon.org/

Pennsylvania
http://www.cwds.pa.gov/cwdsonline

Rhode Island
http://www.employri.org

South Carolina
http://www.sces.org/

South Dakota

http://dlr.sd.gov/

Tennessee
http://www.jobs4tn.gov

Texas
https://wit.twc.state.tx.us

Utah
http://jobs.utah.gov/

Vermont
http://www.vermontjoblink.com/

Virginia
http://www.vec.virginia.gov/find-a-job

Washington
http://www.wa.gov/esd

West Virginia
http://www.wvcommerce.org/business/workforcewv

Wisconsin
https://jobcenterofwisconsin.com/

Wyoming
https://http://www.wyomingatwork.com

www.ingramcontent.com/pod-product-compliance
Lightning Source LLC
Chambersburg PA
CBHW020924180526
45163CB00007B/2879